Every Saturday is parade day.

1

The parade goes right
through my house!

Everyone in my family
marches. We all wear our
favorite parade clothes.

I bang on a tin pan.

My sister toots her trumpet.

Mom waves to the crowd as
we march by. Behind her is a
parade float!

Dad carries our special
parade flag.

The flag says, "Happy Saturday!"